Smart Girl

Yoga for BRAIN POWER

by Rebecca Rissman

CAPSTONE PRESS
a capstone imprint

Savvy Books is published by Capstone Press.
1710 Roe Crest Drive, North Mankato, Minnesota 56003
www.capstonepub.com

Library of Congress Cataloging-in-Publication Data

Cataloging-in-Publication Data is on file with the Library of Congress

ISBN 978-1-4914-2119-2 (library binding)
ISBN 978-1-4914-2360-8 (ebook PDF)

Editorial Credits

Mandy Robbins, editor; Heidi Thompson, designer; Sarah Schuette, prop preparation; Marcy Morin, scheduler; Charmaine Whitman, production specialist

Photo Credits

Capstone Studio: TJ Thoraldson Digital Photography, all photos except; Capstone Studio: Karon Dubke, 7 (top); iStockphoto, Inc: arekmalang, 3 (right top), Di_Studio, 60-61, kaanbelek, 3 (right bottom), manley009, 9 (top); Shutterstock: arek_malang, 4, B Calkins, 7 (bottom), Debby Wong, 59, MANDY GODBEHEAR, 6-7, Monkey Business Images, 58, Photobac, 9 (bottom), Rasstock, 57

Design Elements

Shutterstock: A-R-T, redstone, vectorkat

Printed in Canada.
092014   008478FRS15

TABLE OF Contents

USING *Yoga* to BOOST your BRAIN POWER

You're already pretty smart. Want to boost your G.P.A. even more? Instead of heading to the library to study, you might want to try yoga. That's right, put down your calculator and drop your dictionary. Grab a bottle of water and get started. Practicing yoga is a fun and easy way to build some mental muscle.

Yoga usually involves three elements—yoga poses, meditation, and controlled breathing. Doing yoga poses works your brain because it forces you to concentrate on your alignment in each pose. Meditation also helps your brain. Meditation is the practice of focusing the mind on one thought or idea for several minutes at a time. Controlled breathing in yoga is often called *pranayama*. It requires you to think carefully about every breath you take. Combined, these elements can create the ultimate workout for your brain. Even practicing yoga for just 20 minutes can help you improve your focus, learn new things, and think more clearly.

Some yoga poses are especially beneficial for your brain. Poses that stretch and work the muscles in your back and spine can make you feel energized and ready to learn. Backbends, twists, and inversions are all great for building your mental strength. Incorporating these types of poses into your yoga practice will make sure that you're working your brain as well as the rest of your body.

Yoga Mats

One helpful yoga prop is a yoga mat. It is a long, thin rectangle made of a sticky material such as rubber. Yoga mats are useful because they can help keep your hands and feet from slipping when you get sweaty. You can certainly do yoga without a yoga mat, though. Any flat surface will do, as long as it's not slippery.

Yoga Strap

A yoga strap is a simple but useful yoga prop. Yoga straps can be used to help modify poses. They can help you extend your reach if you're not quite flexible enough to perform the full version of a pose. For example, if you're not able to touch your toes in a forward fold, hook the strap across the balls of your feet and enjoy the stretch.

HOW DO YOU
MEDITATE?

Stop what you're doing. Now empty your mind and sit still for the next hour.

Simple, right? Not so fast.

Meditation is a huge challenge, even for the smartest girls. But don't worry. Anyone can learn to meditate. And once you've developed a regular meditation practice, you'll see huge benefits. You'll be less stressed and anxious. You will learn more quickly and have a better memory. You might even be able to sleep better at night.

There are many different ways to meditate, and all of them are valuable. You can choose to meditate on a loud, busy school bus or in a quiet space. You can meditate alone or in a group, guided or on your own. But the goal of meditation is always the same—to be very still and let your mind be free of thoughts.

Try this out—find a quiet place, such as your bedroom. Clear a space on the floor and sit in a comfortable position. Close your eyes and listen to the sound your breath makes as you inhale and exhale. Try your best not to think about anything else. When your mind begins to wander, do your best to focus it on the noise you make while breathing.

Don't be discouraged if you find yourself accidentally starting to think about homework or an upcoming dance. Just recommit to focusing on the sound of your breath. Do this for as long as you can. When you find that you can't focus, take a break. Your first meditation might last only a minute or two. After time, you could meditate for an hour or even longer.

Try not to fidget. Sit as still as you can while you meditate.

A *Workout* FOR YOUR *Brain*

Yoga mat? Check.

Water bottle? Check.

Brain? Check?

You might not have a choice about whether or not you bring your brain to yoga. But you do have a choice about how you use it. Yoga teachers often talk about being mindful in yoga. This means thinking carefully about what you're doing and not allowing yourself to be distracted by other thoughts and worries. Try your best to focus your thoughts only on your yoga poses and the sound of your breath. This kind of focus is very difficult. But it's a great way to challenge your brain.

Prana

Pronounced: PRAH-nah

From the root *an*, which means "to breathe" and *pra*, which means "forth"

Prana is a Sanskrit word that is used to describe the air that we breathe. However, it is also often interpreted as the energy, or life force, that sustains all living things. Therefore, *prana* is commonly referred to as the "breath of life."

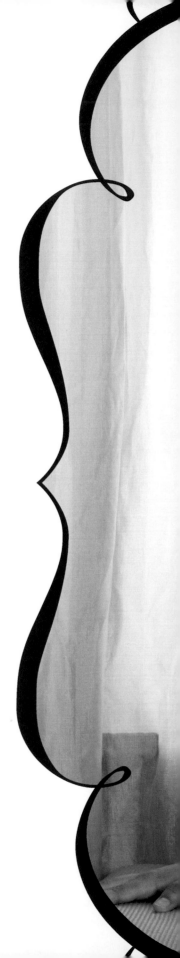

CAT-COW POSE

Cat-Cow Pose is actually a flowing repetition of two separate poses. In Cat Pose, your body will make the shape of a scared cat with an arched back. In Cow Pose, your body will look a bit like a cow with a heavy belly. These two poses work the muscles in your core, back, and neck. Moving back and forth between the poses works your brain as you concentrate on keeping proper form.

step 1 Start on your hands and knees. Make sure your knees are directly under your hips, and your hands are directly under your shoulders.

step 2 Spread your fingers wide. Press all parts of your palms down into the mat, and straighten your elbows.

step 3 As you inhale, drop your belly button down toward the mat and lift your gaze. Point your tailbone up. This is Cow Pose.

step 4   As you exhale, pull your belly button in toward your spine as you point your tailbone down. Tuck your chin into your chest, and press your shoulder blades away from one another. Lift the center of your back up into Cat Pose.

step 5   As you inhale, repeat Step 3. As you exhale, repeat Step 4. Do this at least five times. Try to make each movement last as long as each breath.

EXTENDED PUPPY POSE

Sanskrit Name: *Uttana Shishosana*

Pronounced: OOH-tah-nah sheesh-oh-SAH-nah

Have you ever seen a dog wake up and stretch, sticking its tail in the air? In this pose, you'll imitate Fido's favorite stretch. Extended Puppy Pose will energize the spine, neck, and arms and get blood flowing to your brain.

step 1 Start on your hands and knees. Make sure your knees are directly under your hips.

step 2 Walk your hands about one handprint forward. Try to press all parts of your palms down into the mat equally.

step 3 Point your tailbone up as you bring your forehead to the mat. If you aren't able to comfortably rest your forehead on the mat, rest it on a folded blanket.

Yoga blankets are thick, soft props that can be useful in many different poses. Folded, rolled, or laid flat, yoga blankets can be used to make poses easier or more comfortable. Fold a yoga blanket into a long rectangle and place it under your forehead in Extended Puppy Pose for a slightly easier version of this stretch.

step 4 Allow your belly to gently fall toward the mat until you feel a slight back bend.

step 5 Hold for a few breaths. Then return to your hands and knees to rest.

Keep a straight line from your hip to your knee.

REVERSE NAMASTE

Reverse Namaste is an excellent stretch for your shoulders, neck, and mind. Yes, you read that correctly. A yoga pose can stretch your mind! First you need to focus your mental energies on finding this position correctly. Then you'll need to work hard to stay focused as you breathe deeply and sit peacefully in this pose.

step 1 Sit on your mat with your shins crossed comfortably. Rock briefly from side to side until you have evenly distributed your weight across both sides of your bottom.

step 2 Straighten your back by lifting the crown of your head straight up. Lift your chin slightly to make your jaw parallel to the floor.

step 3 Bring both arms out to your sides with your palms facing down. Drop your shoulders away from your ears.

step 4 Bring your palms together behind your back with your fingertips pointing up. Pull your hands upward until they are between your shoulder blades. Try to press all parts of your hands together.

step 5 Hold for a few breaths.

If bringing the palms together is too difficult, try making two fists and pressing the knuckles of each hand together.

Mudra

Pronounced: MOO-drah

From the root *mud*, which means "joy" and *ra*, which means "to give"

Mudras are special hand positions. Some people believe that mudras help people to hold the source of their energy. One of the most common mudras is called anjeli mudra. It is performed by placing the palms together in front of the heart with the fingers pointing up.

EASY POSE

Sanskrit Name: *Sukhasana*

Pronounced: soo-CAWS-ah-nah

Easy Pose is a great pose for when you meditate. Think carefully about your alignment in this pose. Don't allow your body to slouch or lean forward.

step 1 Sit on your mat or a folded yoga blanket. Rock from side to side briefly to make sure you are resting evenly on both sides of your bottom.

step 2 Cross your shins and allow your knees to fall out to the sides. Relax the muscles in your feet until the outer edges of your feet rest on the mat.

step 3 Drop your shoulders away from your ears. Allow your hands to rest comfortably on top of your thighs. You can rest your hands palm-down on your thighs. You could also have your palms facing up with your fingers in a mudra. One common mudra used in this pose is to have your index finger and thumb touch, with the rest of your fingers extended down.

step 4 Sit up very tall with your back as straight as possible. Make sure your shoulders are above your hips. Lift your chin slightly so that your jaw is parallel to the floor.

step 5 Hold for at least one minute.

➤ Don't let the name of this pose fool you! Easy Pose is actually quite difficult to hold. It works the muscles in your neck, back, and abdomen.

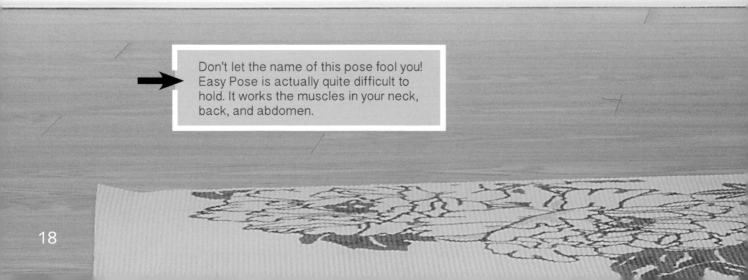

REVOLVED WIDE-LEGGED FORWARD FOLD

Sanskrit Name: *Parivrtta Prasarita Padottanasana*

Pronounced: par-VREE-tah prah-sah-REE-tah pah-doh-tah-NAHS-ah-nah

Are you feeling down or bored? Give yourself a healthy head rush to perk right up. The muscles in your legs, feet, and back will get a great workout too.

step 1 Stand in the middle of your mat.

step 2 Take a big step out to the right so that your feet are at least 3 feet (1 meter) apart. Have your toes slightly closer together than your heels.

step 3 Bring your hands to your hips.

step 4 Put a slight bend in your knees and bend at the hips to fold forward.

step 5 If you can, slowly straighten your knees. If this feels too intense, keep a slight bend in your knees.

step 6 Bring your right hand down to the mat directly under your heart. Straighten your right elbow.

step 7 Reach your left arm straight up into the air.

step 8 Keeping your hips level to the ground, twist your upper body open to the left. Try your best to stack your left shoulder above your right so that they form a vertical line.

step 9 Hold for a few breaths.

step 10 Repeat on the other side.

FISH POSE

Sanskrit Name: *Matsyasana*

Pronunciation: mot-see-AHS-ah-nah

According to an ancient Indian text, Fish Pose is called the "destroyer of all diseases." While it may not cure disease, practicing this pose regularly will certainly help put you in the right state of mind. This pose stretches and strengthens the muscles in your neck, abdomen, and arms. It also places your heart above your head, which helps more blood reach the brain.

step 1 Lie on your back. Bend your knees up and rest your feet on the mat.

step 2 Lift your hips slightly off the mat and slide both hands, palms facing down, underneath your bottom. Bring your bottom down on top of your hands.

step 3 Keeping your elbows and forearms close to the sides of your body, lift your upper chest and head away from the mat. Imagine someone is lifting you up from the center of your chest.

step 4 Release your head backward. Either let it hang while you look behind you, or allow the top of your head to rest onto the mat.

step 5 One at a time, straighten your legs out in front of you. Flex your feet and keep your thighs squeezing toward one another.

step 6 Hold for a few breaths.

step 7 To release from this pose, lift your head away from the floor by looking up. Slowly lower your back and head down onto the mat.

Flex your feet.

LOGS ON FIRE POSE

Sanskrit Name: *Agnistambhasana*

Pronunciation: ah-nee-stahm-BAHS-ah-nah

When you are in the correct alignment in this pose, your shins are stacked on top of each other, just like two logs in a fire. This pose is an excellent stretch for the hips and will also energize the spine, neck, and brain.

step 1   Sit in Easy Pose with your right shin crossed in front of your left.

step 2   Bring your left ankle on top of your right knee. Flex your left foot to point your toes directly in front of you.

step 3   Inch your right ankle forward on the mat so that it is directly under your left knee. You might need to reach down and use your hands to help move it into the right position. The bones of your shins should be parallel to one another. Flex both feet.

step 4   Lift the crown of your head to sit up very straight. Lift your chin slightly to make your jaw parallel to the floor.

step 5   Bring your fingertips to the mat on either side of your hips. Hold for a few breaths.

step 6   Repeat on the other side.

Flex your feet ——————

Keep your
shins parallel
to the floor.

HEAD-TO-KNEE POSE

Sanskrit Name: *Janu Sirsasana*

Pronounced: jah-NOO sheer-SHAHS-ah-nah

Head-to-Knee Pose combines a deep forward fold with a hip stretch. It lengthens the muscles in your legs, but also helps you relax the muscles in your neck, back, and shoulders. Releasing tension from these muscle groups can help you feel focused and ready to learn. Remember not to lock your knee while doing this pose. Locking your knee can lead to overstretching and possibly injuring your muscles.

step 1 Sit on your mat with both legs extended in front of you.

step 2 Bend your right knee and pull the sole of your right foot into the inside of your left thigh. Allow your right knee to fall out to the right. If this feels like too much of a stretch, allow your right thigh to rest on a yoga blanket or a pillow.

step 3 Flex your left foot to point the toes straight up.

step 4 Sit up very tall. Center your upper body over your extended left leg by pointing your belly button at your left knee.

step 5 Keeping your hands on either side of the left leg, start to walk them forward toward your left foot. Stop when you feel the stretch.

step 6 Hold for a few breaths.

step 7 Repeat on the other side.

Flex your foot.

SUPPORTED HEADSTAND

Sanskrit Name: *Salamba Sirsasana*

Pronounced: sah-LAHM-bah seer-SAHS-ah-nah

Feeling drowsy? Homework got you down? Instead of reaching for an energy drink, try an inversion instead. Inversions such as the Supported Headstand are yoga poses that bring your head below your heart. Doing an inversion for just a few breaths can give you a healthy jolt of energy.

step 1 Bring your mat to a clear, empty wall. Don't choose a wall that has windows or anything hanging on it that you might break or knock down.

step 2 Come to your hands and knees facing the wall.

step 3 Bring your elbows down onto the mat, shoulder-distance apart. Interlace your fingers. Your knuckles should be a few inches from the wall.

step 4 Tuck your toes under and lift your knees off the mat. Stick your bottom up into the air.

step 5 Slowly start to walk your feet in toward your elbows. Try to keep your knees as straight as you can.

step 6 Press your forearms down into the mat. When you have walked forward far enough, your shoulders will be right above your elbows. Pause and hold this for a few breaths.

28

continue on page 30 ➡

If straightening your knees is very challenging for you, or if you feel this stretch intensely in your shoulders, work on Step 5 without moving on. You will still get all the benefits of this pose, but you won't risk injuring yourself.

SUPPORTED HEADSTAND
continued

step 7   Slowly lower your head down onto the mat. Keep pressing into your forearms.

step 8   Lift your right leg straight up into the air. Keep your knee straight.

step 9   Bend your left leg deeply. With control, spring off of your left foot to hop your right foot toward the wall. Be patient with yourself. This step might take a few tries.

Use control when kicking up into a headstand. You do not want to crash into the wall. Rather, the wall is there to lightly support you and keep you in the correct alignment. Your feet should gently tap the wall.

Flex your feet.

step 10 When your right foot makes contact with the wall, use the muscles in your abdomen to swing your left leg up against the wall as well.

step 11 Bring your legs together. Flex your feet so that it looks like you're trying to stand on the ceiling.

step 12 Pull your belly button in toward your spine.

step 13 Hold for a few breaths.

step 14 Bring your right foot down to the mat. Then bring your left foot down as well. Rest on your hands and knees.

step 15 Repeat, leading with the opposite leg.

Stay safe! Keep pressing into your forearms when you are upside down in Supported Headstand. You should only have a small amount of weight resting on your head. Your arms can support the rest of your weight.

SHOULDER STAND

Sanskrit Name: *Salambba Sarvangasana*

Pronounced: sah-LAHM-bah sar-vahn-GAHS-ah-nah

Have you ever heard someone talk about a head rush? Well, doing Shoulder Stand is a great way to get a brain rush! This inversion encourages blood to flow to the head, neck, and heart. The increased blood flow can help wake you up and energize your mind. Beginners might hold this pose for a few breaths, but advanced yoga students often stay in Shoulder Stand for a minute or more.

A yoga blanket is helpful in Shoulder Stand because it can prevent you from overstretching the back of your neck. Yoga blankets are thin wool blankets. But any blanket can be used as a prop—as long as you don't mind it getting a little sweaty.

step 1 Fold a yoga blanket to make a rectangle that is about 2 feet (0.6 m) long by 1 foot (0.3 m) across. Place the folded blanket on your mat. Lay down on it so that the blanket supports your shoulders but your head rests on the mat.

step 2 Bring your arms down to your sides with your palms facing down. Bend your knees up and bring your feet onto the mat just in front of your bottom.

step 3 Use the muscles of your abdomen to pull your knees into your chest.

step 2

step 4 To move into the inversion, press your arms down into the mat. Use the muscles of your abdomen to lift your hips and torso off the mat. Curl your torso to reach your knees toward your face, and bring most of your weight onto your shoulder blades.

step 5 Bend your elbows, and bring your hands to your lower back with your fingers pointing toward your heels. Try to keep your elbows from splaying out to the sides.

continue on next page ➡

SHOULDER STAND
continued

step 6   Using your hands as support, slowly straighten your legs up. Try to make your legs rise straight up, so that they are perpendicular to the mat.

step 7   Press the back of your head down into the mat to make space between your chin and your chest.

step 8   Press the balls of your feet up. Keep your legs together.

step 9   Hold for a few breaths.

step 10 There are two ways to exit this pose. The first is to bend your knees and pull them in toward your face. Then straighten your arms down onto the mat, palms facing down. Very slowly roll onto your back and rest. The second way to exit this pose is to take Plow Pose.

Plow Pose

PLOW POSE

Sanskrit Name: *Halasana*
Pronounced: hall-AHS-ah-nah

Sit on the floor and reach your head toward your toes. Now imagine flipping that stretch upside down, and you've got Plow Pose. This pose stretches the back, legs, and neck while it works the muscles in your core.

step 1   Start in Shoulder Stand.

Shoulder Stand

step 2   With your elbows bent and your hands supporting your lower back, begin to lower your feet toward the mat behind your head. Keep your legs as straight as possible.

Step 2

step 3 Bring your feet as close to the mat as you can. They might rest on the mat behind your head, or they might hover off the ground. Don't worry about where they are. Instead, think about the deep stretch you're feeling in your back and legs.

step 4 Straighten your arms onto the mat. Interlace your hands and press your wrists and elbows down into the mat.

step 5 Hold for a few breaths.

step 6 Unclasp your hands, and press your palms down into the mat.

step 7 Slowly roll onto your back. Rest for a few breaths.

Plow Pose can be a very intense stretch. Remember to come into the pose slowly and stop if you feel any pain.

REVOLVED CHAIR POSE

Sanskrit Name: *Parivrtta Utkatasana*

Pronunciation: par-VREET-ah ooht-kah-TAHS-ah-nah

Energizing the muscles around your spine is a sure way to wake up your brain. The deep spinal twist in Revolved Chair Pose stretches the muscles in your neck, core, and back too. Feel free to make this pose as challenging as you want by adjusting the amount you twist.

step 1 Stand at the top of your mat with your big toes touching and your heels slightly separated.

step 2 Bring your palms together in front of your heart.

step 3 Bend your knees deeply as though you were about to sit down in a chair. Keep your knees together.

step 4 Twist your upper body open to the right. Bring your left elbow to the outside of your right knee. Keep pressing your palms together.

step 5 Look up over your right shoulder.

step 6 Hold for a few breaths. Keep your weight evenly spread across both feet and squeeze your knees together.

step 7 Return to a standing position to rest. Repeat on the other side.

If this twist is too challenging, modify it by bringing your left elbow to the outside of your left knee. If you want to make this pose more difficult, try bringing your left fingertips to the outside of your right foot and reach your right hand up.

REVOLVED HIGH LUNGE POSE

Here's another spinal twist to boost your mental mojo and burn fat while building muscle. Try the basic version of this pose first, but then feel free to try different variations.

step 1 From a standing position, take a big step forward with your left leg. Point your left toes straight ahead.

step 2 Bend the left knee deeply while you keep your right leg as straight as you can. Lift your right heel away from the floor so that you are resting on the ball of your right foot.

step 3 Bring your palms together in front of your heart.

step 4 Twist your upper body open to the left. Bring your right elbow to the outside of your left knee. Keep pressing your palms together.

step 5 Keep your right leg very straight. Lift your chin away from your chest to lengthen your back.

step 6 Hold for a few breaths.

step 7 Repeat on the other side.

! You can keep the challenging twist while gaining more stability. Just touch your right hand to the floor just outside your left foot.

Does this twist feel too intense? Try keeping your right hand on the mat on the inside of your left foot and simply lift your left hand up.

STAFF POSE

Sanskrit Name: *Dandasana*

Pronunciation: don-DAHS-ah-nah

Staff Pose is much more intense than it looks. This pose works the muscles of your core, neck, and legs. You'll need to focus to make your back as straight as possible in this pose. If the muscles in your back become tired quickly, it means you're getting a good workout.

step 1 Sit on your mat with your legs outstretched. Rock from side to side briefly to make sure you are resting evenly on both sides of your bottom.

step 2 With your legs together, flex your feet to point your toes straight up. Engage the muscles in your thighs to pull your kneecaps toward your hips.

Drop your shoulders and lengthen your neck.

Keep your back straight.

step 3 Bring your hands down to your sides with your elbows straight. Rest your fingertips or palms on the mat.

step 4 Pull your shoulders down away from your ears.

step 5 Pull your belly button in toward your spine.

step 6 Sit as upright as possible. To do this, bring your shoulders back so that they are directly above your hips.

step 7 Lift your chin slightly so that your jaw is parallel to the floor. Hold for a few breaths.

If it is very difficult for you to bring your back completely upright, try altering this pose slightly. Sit on a folded yoga blanket to bring your hips a bit off the floor.

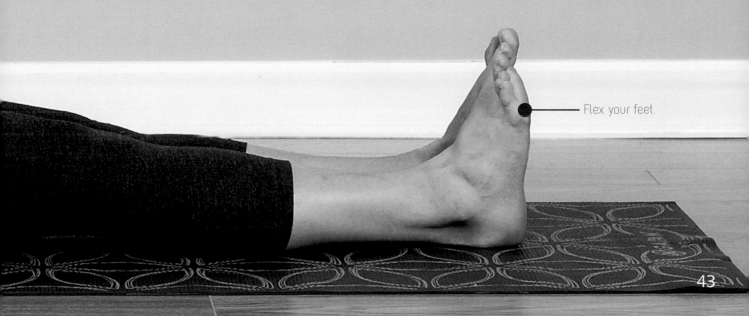

Flex your feet.

HALF-LOTUS FORWARD FOLD

Sanskrit Name: *Ardha Baddha Paschimottanasana*

Pronunciation: ARE-dah BAH-dah pah-shee-moe-tah-NAHS-ah-nah

Many people respond to stress or anxiety by tensing their muscles. When you are stressed, concentrating and learning can be very difficult. Poses such as Half-Lotus Forward Fold help release unwanted tension so that you can focus your mind.

Step 1

step 1 Sit on your mat with your legs outstretched.

Step 2

step 2 Bend your left knee up and pull your left heel in toward your bottom

step 3 Bring the top of your left foot to the top of your right hip. The sole of your left foot will face up.

Step 4

Flex your feet.

step 4 Allow your left knee to fall open to the left. If this is too much of a stretch on your right knee and hip, place a folded yoga blanket under the left knee.

step 5 Keep the right leg straight and flex the foot so that the right toes point straight up.

step 6 Bring your hands to the mat on either side of your hips. Inhale and straighten your back as much as you can.

step 7 As you exhale, bend at the hips to fold forward. Keep in mind this might be a very small movement and you might not bend very far.

step 8 Hold for a few breaths.

step 9 Repeat on the other side.

If it is very difficult for you to bring your back completely upright, try altering this pose slightly. Sit on a folded yoga blanket to bring your hips a bit off the floor.

LOTUS POSE

Sanskrit Name: *Padmasana*

Pronunciation: pahd-mah-NAHS-ah-nah

Lotus Pose is one of yoga's most famous poses. But it's also one of the most difficult. It works the muscles of the back and gives you a very deep stretch in the hips. Be patient with yourself while you learn this pose. Focus on breathing slowly and deeply while you are in Lotus Pose. One day, you might be able to meditate for hours while in this pose.

step 1 Sit on your mat with your legs outstretched. Rock from side to side to distribute the weight evenly across both sides of your bottom.

step 2 Bend your left knee out to the side and bring the top of your left foot to the top of your right thigh. The sole of your left foot will face up.

step 3 Bend your right knee, and bring your right ankle in front of your left knee. Hold this for a few breaths. If this feels challenging, remain in this pose.

step 4 If you want more of a challenge, use your hands to bring the top of your right foot to the top of your left thigh. The sole of the foot will face up.

step 5 Sit up very straight by bringing your shoulders directly above your hips.

 If Step 3 feels too intense, place a folded yoga blanket under your right knee for support.

step 6 Rest your hands on your thighs with your palms facing up. Bring your thumb and index finger together to form a mudra.

step 7 Hold for a few breaths.

step 8 Repeat crossing the legs in the opposite way.

SEATED FORWARD BEND

Sanskrit Name: *Paschimottonasana*

Pronunciation: pah-shee-moh-ta-NAHS-ah-nah

Are your legs and brain ready for a good stretch? The Seated Forward Bend will really challenge your legs, but that's not all. Keeping your thoughts focused in yoga can be difficult. This forward fold is a great time to work on calming your thoughts and growing your mental muscle.

step 1 Sit on your mat with your legs outstretched. Rock from side to side to distribute your weight evenly across both sides of your bottom.

step 2 Flex your feet so that your toes point straight up. Engage the muscles in your legs to pull your knees toward your hips.

step 4

step 3 Reach your arms up. Straighten your back and lift your rib cage up away from your hips.

step 4 Keeping as much lift in your upper body as you can, bend at the hips to fold forward. Reach your hands to your knees, shins, or the outer edges of your feet.

step 5 Inhale deeply and lift your head and chest slightly as you straighten your back as much as you can.

step 6 Exhale and fold forward deeply, allowing your back to round a bit as you stretch the crown of your head toward the tops of your feet.

step 7 Hold for a few breaths.

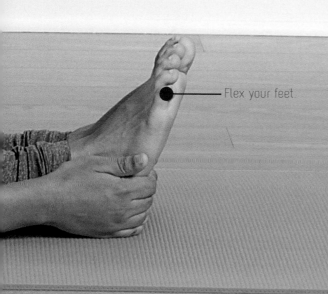

Flex your feet.

BOUND STANDING FORWARD FOLD

How often do you think about your hard-working shoulder muscles? This variation on Standing Forward Fold will give them just the stretch they need.

step 1 Stand at the top of your mat with your feet slightly wider than hips-distance apart.

step 2 Interlace your fingers behind your back. Straighten your elbows as much as you can by pressing your knuckles toward the floor.

step 3 Put a small bend in your knees.

step 4 Bend at the hips to fold forward. Bring your knuckles up.

step 5 As you relax your neck and shoulders, try to bring your knuckles toward the front of your mat. Keep your elbows very straight.

If it's hard to interlace your fingers, just hold on to a towel or yoga strap.

step 6 If this position feels like a good challenge, hold it for a few breaths. If you want to make this pose more difficult, begin to straighten your knees.

step 7 Hold for a few breaths.

THREAD THE NEEDLE POSE

Deep spinal twists are one of the best ways to wake up your body and mind. But if you're looking to rest your body while waking up your mind, Thread the Needle Pose will come in handy. This twist allows you to rest on the floor while you do it.

step 1 Start on your hands and knees. Tuck your toes under on the mat.

step 2 Lift your right hand and "thread it" under your left to bring your right shoulder onto the center of the mat.

step 3 Face your right palm up. Press all parts of your right arm and shoulder into the mat.

step 4 Keep both knees pressing evenly into the mat. Try to keep your left hip from rising higher than your right.

step 5 Hold for a few breaths.

step 6 Repeat on the other side.

Karma

Pronounced: CAR-mah

From the root *Kri* meaning, "to act"

Have you ever heard someone say, "What goes around comes around?" You might not have realized it, but they were talking about an ancient Indian idea called *Karma*. Karma is the idea that the actions we commit in the past can affect the things that happen to us in the future. Karma is a good reminder to be kind to others and yourself in the present. It's also a good principle to remember in your yoga practice. Respect your body and muscles, and you'll enjoy good health later in life. Exercise carelessly or in a dangerous way, and your injuries could make life difficult for you later on!

LEG LIFTS

Sanskrit Name: *Urdhva Prasarita Padasana*

Pronunciation: OOR-dvah prah-sah-REE-tah pah-DAHS-ah-nah

Stretching and strengthening your back is a quick, natural way to safely energize your whole body. But don't forget to give some attention to the muscles of your core too. A strong core will help you avoid back injuries over time, and it will also make your spinal stretches more effective.

Use your breath to flow between the different positions described in this pose. Over time, as your core becomes stronger, you might experiment with holding your legs at different heights.

step 1 Lie on your back with your legs outstretched.

step 2 Reach your arms over your head with your palms facing up.

step 3 Exhale deeply as you use the muscles in your core to lift your feet halfway up. Keep pressing the backs of your hands into the floor. Hold for a few breaths.

step 4 Exhale again, and lift your feet all the way up until they are above your hips. Hold for a few breaths.

step 5 Lower your legs all the way to the floor to rest.

step 6 Repeat Steps 3 and 4 a few times.

Try to lift your legs to a complete right angle.

READING ABOUT

Yoga

Now that your mind is primed, you might want to use those extra sharp brain cells to learn a bit more about where the ancient practice of yoga comes from. While we know that yoga is very old, it is actually quite difficult to point to its specific origins. We can, however, identify some of its general sources. The philosophy that guides yoga comes from several places, including eastern religious belief systems such as Hinduism, Taosim, Buddhism, and Jainism. Some ancient texts have also had a large impact on the development of yoga. If you're interested, check out these books online or in the library:

- The Bhagavad Gita: an ancient Indian collection of yoga scriptures

- Tao de Ching: an ancient Chinese guide to how to think about life

- Yoga Sutras of Patanjali: an ancient Indian collection of truths about life and yoga

Yoga teachers often talk about characters from the Bhagavad Gita, or thoughts from the Tao de Ching or Yoga Sutras during their classes. Learning more about these ancient texts can make your yoga practice more fun and rewarding.

Is Yoga Religious?

Even though many of yoga's roots come from eastern religions, very few Americans practice yoga for religious reasons.

56

Away from the library? No problem! The Internet is overflowing with great yoga resources. Websites such as *Yoga Journal* feature in-depth articles about yoga poses, yoga philosophy, and the history of yoga. Yoga blogs are also great informal places to learn about yoga. You can read about how people practice yoga and how they incorporate yoga into their lives. Many yoga blogs even feature instructional photos.

Ask a trusted adult to help you find a yoga blog that uses multimedia, such as photos and videos.

Celebrities and Yoga

Yoga lovers even include celebrities. Adam Levine, Madonna, Ashley Tisdale, Vanessa Hudgens, Jennifer Aniston, and Giselle Bundchen all practice yoga. While many celebrities talk about the physical benefits of yoga, some are also vocal about how yoga has helped their minds.

BRINGING YOGA WITH YOU *Anywhere*

You're running out the door for school. You're juggling your backpack, breakfast, and a stack of library books that you're pretty sure are overdue. Your brother is yelling something, but you ignore him because you can't remember whether you grabbed your homework off the printer upstairs. Sound familiar?

Stop. Close your eyes. Breathe.

Slow down and think about the things you're doing the same way you think about a yoga pose. Take everything one step at a time. If you have a mantra, say it to yourself. When you are able to slow down, you will think more clearly and be less likely to forget something.

The more you practice mindfulness in yoga, the easier it will be to practice it in your life. Remember how you feel at the end of a good yoga workout, and do your best to bring that feeling with you into the rest of the day.

Mantra

Pronounced: MOHN-trah

From the root *man*, which means "to think" and *tra*, which means "instrumental"

A mantra is a word or phrase that has special meaning. One of the most common mantras is the sound "*om.*" Some people chant or repeat their mantra over and over to help them concentrate or meditate.

Glossary

alignment (uh-LINE-muhnt)—the correct positioning of the body in order to reduce the chance of injury

inversion (in-VUR-shuhn)—a type of pose in which the head is brought below the heart; standing forward folds, headstands, and handstands are all considered inversions

meditate (MED-i-tayt)—to think deeply and quietly

mudra (MOO-druh)—a special hand position

prop (PROP)—a tool used to make different yoga poses easier

Sanskrit (SAN-skrit)—an ancient language from India written from left to right in a script called Devangari

torso (TOR-soh)—the part of the body between the neck and waist, not including the arms

READ MORE

Burns, Brian, Howard Kent, and Claire Hayler. *Yoga for Beginners.* From Couch to Conditioned: A Beginner's Guide to Getting Fit. New York: Rosen Pub., 2011.

Purperhart, Helen. *Yoga Exercises for Teens: Developing a Calmer Mind and a Stronger Body.* Alameda, Calif.: Hunter House Publishers, 2009.

Spilling, Michael, and Liz Lark. *Yoga Step-By-Step.* Skills in Motion. New York: Rosen Central, 2011.

Wood, Alix. *You Can Do Yoga.* Let's Get Moving! Gareth Stevens Publishing: New York, 2014.

INTERNET SITES

FactHound offers a safe, fun way to find Internet sites related to this book. All of the sites on FactHound have been researched by our staff.

Here's all you do:

Visit *www.facthound.com*

Type in this code: 9781491421192

ABOUT THE AUTHOR

Rebecca Rissman is a certified yoga instructor, nonfiction author, and editor. She has written books about history, culture, science, and art. Her book *Shapes in Sports* earned a starred review from *Booklist* magazine, and her series *Animal Spikes and Spines* received *Learning Magazine*'s 2013 Teachers Choice for Children's Books. She lives in Portland, Oregon, with her husband and daughter, and enjoys hiking, yoga, and cooking.

Index